Baby of the Country Stars

Paul Randall

Union and Confederacy Incorporated
P. O. Box 11
College Grove, Tennessee 37046

Photo Credits

Bernard Boudreau
    page 185 upper left
Peter Brill
    page 153 lower right
Cathy Burkey
    page 190 upper left
Anthony Darius
    page 187 lower right
Dean Dixon
    page 156 lower left
    page 169 upper right
    page 178 upper left
    page 189 lower left
Leonard Kamsler
    page 168 upper left
Ron Keith/Scott Bonner
    page 155 lower right
    page 160 upper left
Bill King
    page 171 upper left
Harry Langdon
    page 155 upper left
    page 176 upper left
McGuire
    page 156 upper left

Alan Messer
    page 183 lower left
    page 190 upper right
Nash
    page 183 lower right
Randee St. Nicholas
    page 153 upper right
    page 167 lower right
Beverly Parker
    page 156 lower right
    page 165 lower left
    page 168 lower right
    page 179 upper left
Victoria Pearson
    page 186 lower left
Jim and Pat Rawlings
    page 188 upper left
Jack Sallow
    page 179 lower right
Mark Tucker
    page 166 lower left
    page 173 lower left
Ron Williams
    page 164 upper right

Editorial/production supervision and interior design:
Paul C. Wassel Jr. a.k.a. Paul Randall

Cover design and artwork: Cover Photo: Hope Powell
Robert K. Oermann

Printing by K & S Press Inc.—Nashville, Tennessee

Typesetting by Michael Walker

Photo engraving K & S Press

Published by: Union and Confederacy Incorporated
                P. O. Box 11
                College Grove, Tennessee 37046

ISBN 0-911679-01-4   Library of Congress #TX-2-366-758

DEDICATION

To Country Music Fans everywhere.

ACKNOWLEDGMENTS

The baby photos and the current photos in this book were provided by the artists, members of their families, close friends, personal managers, office staffs, booking agents, publicity departments, public relations firms or recording companies.

I wish to thank everyone for their co-operation and dedicated assistance in bringing this four-year project to fruition.

Paul Randall

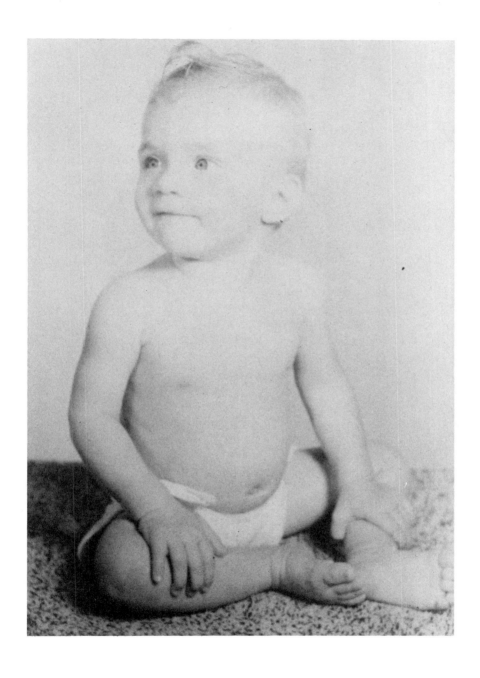

She's six months old here, but much later she was a drummer for her sister's group, The Do-Rites. She also played drums for her on her television show. (See page 153)

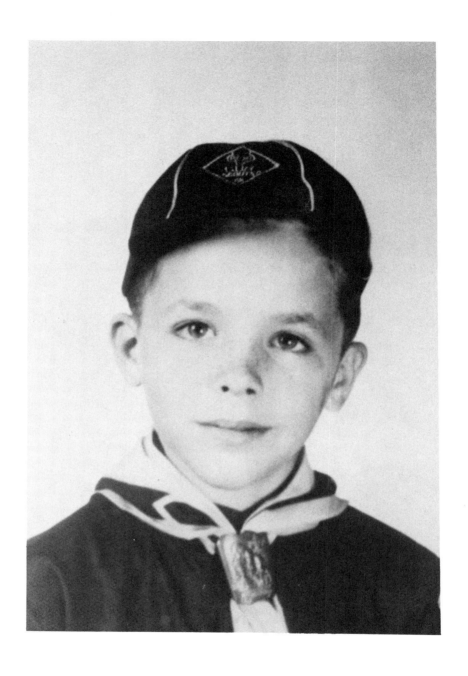

He's an 8 year, 10 month old cub scout here. His hits "Velvet Chains" and "Wind Beneath My Wings" made him a star. (See page 153)

He's 15 months old here. His hometown is Lafayette, Louisiana and his hit "Who Do You Know in California" established his stardom. (See page 153)

He's about 3 years old in this photo. That's him on the right and that's his sister, Virginia Ruth, next to him. Many years later he had a hit called "Love in the Hot Afternoon" that really started his career going. (See page 153)

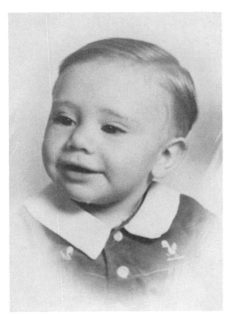

In the striped shirt he's 15 years old and in the other photo he's 5 years old. One of his big hits was "I'm Gonna Hire a Wino To Decorate Our Home." (See page 154)

This is the only young photo to be found of this singer. He's 13 years old here. One of his biggest hits was "Gentle On My Mind." (See page 154)

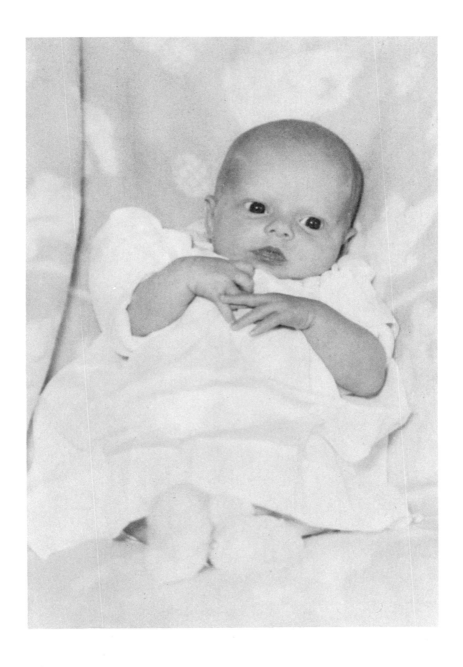

She's just 18 days old in this photo. Although from Ohio, she's known as "The Tennessee Yodeler" now. "Don't Break the Heart That Loves You" was one of her big hits. (See page 154)

She says this is the only photo she had of herself as a child. She's 11 years old here. This Grand Ole Opry Star's autobiography is called "Sunshine and Shadow." (See page 154)

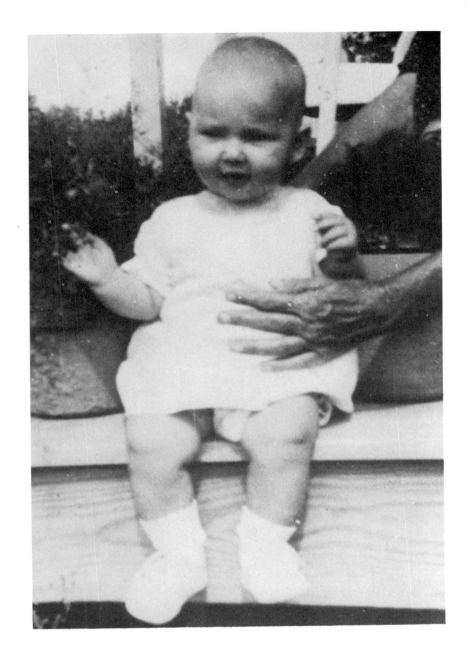

This is her favorite photo of herself as a child. She's 9 months old in it. "Stand By Your Man" should give you her identity. (See page 155)

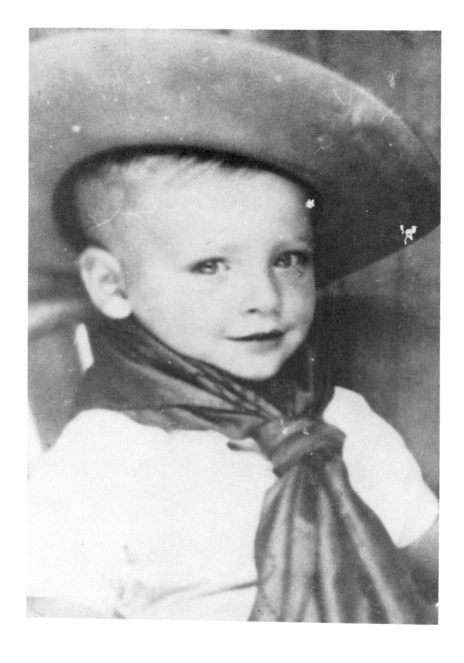

Born in Texas, this 3 year old almost became a Pittsburgh Pirate, but instead gave us "Let's Think About Livin" as one of his biggest hits. (See page 155)

The 4 year old with the hat grew up to host the Nashville Network TV show "You Can Be A Star." He also had some big hits like "Pop-A-Top." That's his older sister, Maxine, and his younger brother, Raymond, in the photo with him. (See page 155)

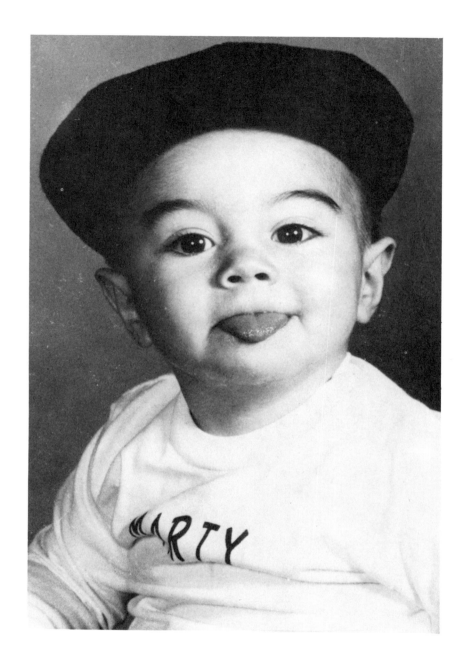

A 2 year old here with his first name on his shirt. 11 years after this photo was taken, he started playing mandolin for Flatt and Scruggs. In the early eighties, his solo album, "Busy Bee Cafe" was widely acclaimed. (See page 155)

This picture shows two/thirds of a famous family trio. "You Put the Blue in Me" and "Ain't No Binds" were two of their hits.

Sharon (left) is 2 years old and Cheryl (right) is 1 year old. (See page 156)

3 months

2 years

Her first big hit was "Delta Dawn". (See page 156)

14

They're 4 years old in this photo. They're identical twins named Jim (left) and John (right). They were featured performers on the "HeeHaw" television show for many years. (See page 156)

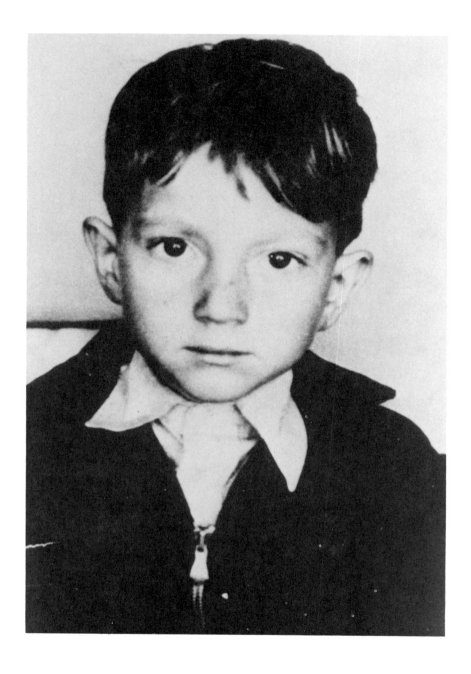

A school picture of him when he was about 4 years old. He didn't start wearing a red bandana till many years later. (See page 156)

16

A singer, songwriter, disc jockey, actor, emcee and television show host are just some of his credits. He was 18 months old when this photo was taken. One of his biggest hits was "Sixteen Tons." (See page 157).

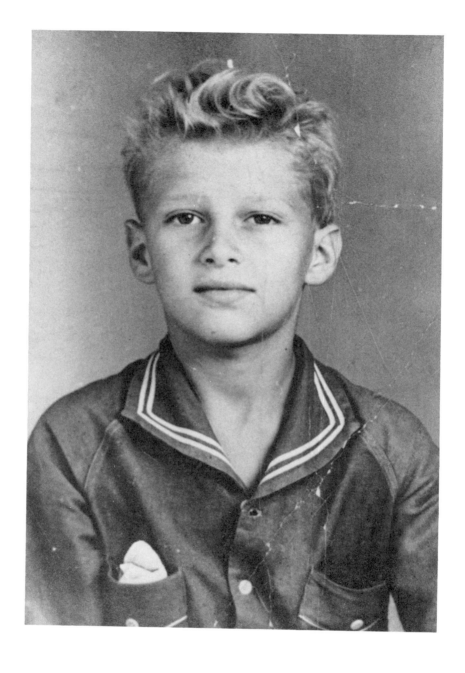

He's 8 years old here and in 1966 joined the Grand Ole Opry as a regular. "Girl on the Billboard" was one of his big hits in 1965. (See page 157)

She's 3 years old above, but now plays rhythm guitar and sings lead.

She's 3 years old in this photo and sings harmony in the duet and is the oldest of the two.

This duet's first number one country record was "Mama He's Crazy." (See page 157)

19

He's a member of the Grand Ole Opry and one of his big hits was "May the Bird of Paradise Fly Up Your Nose." He's 12 years old in the above photos. (See page 157)

He's 3 years old as Davy Crockett and 4 years old on the tractor. "Pass Me By" was his first release on Mercury Records in the early seventies. (See page 158)

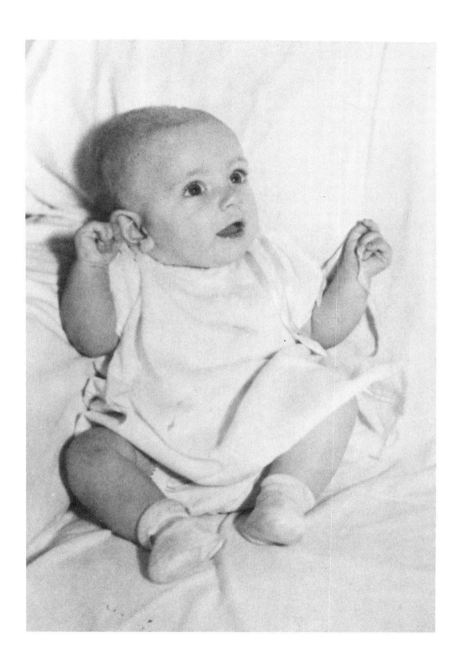

She's a cute little 6 months old here. She began her career at the WWVA Jamboree in Wheeling, West Virginia and soon landed a recording contract in Nashville. One of her hits was "Down in the Boondocks." Early in her career she did some very successful duets with Del Reeves. (See page 158)

In 1968 he was elected into the Country Music Hall of Fame. This photo was taken when he was about 5½ years old. "Old Shep" was one of his big hits. (See page 158)

Even in this photo at 8 years old he looked like a country singer. Oddly enough, his first number one country record was "Games People Play," which happened while he was a member of the Paul Revere and the Raiders rock group. (See page 158).

She's 3 years old here. In 1982 she had country music's *only* gold single. The song was "Nobody." (See page 159)

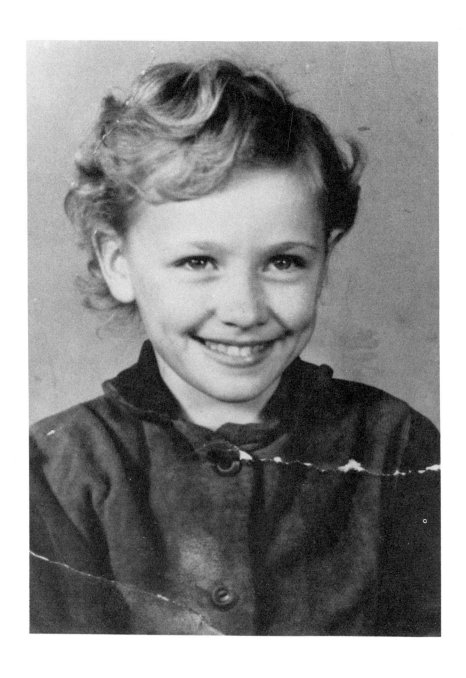

Do you really need a clue to figure out who this is? She's about 9 years old in this
photo. (See page 159)

Bright is his real middle name and he's 10 years old here. As a songwriter, "Act Naturally" was his bright creation and as a singer, "Rednecks, White Socks and Blue Ribbon Beer" made his star bright in the mid-seventies. (See page 159)

She's 3 years old in this picture. She's a native Nashvillian who was one of the 10 nominees for the Top New Female Vocalist in the 1985 Academy of Country Music Awards. (See page 159)

"Raindrops Keep Fallin' on My Head" was one of his big hits. He was 3 years old in this photo. (See page 160)

This little 14 month old guy seems to be enjoying sitting on the hood of that car. Looks like he maybe starting to sing "Baby's Got Her Blue Jeans On," which was one of his hits much later in life. (See page 160)

She won a Grammy for Best Country Vocal Performance in 1970 for her hit "Rose Garden." She was 2 years old when the photo above was taken. (See page 160).

Harold at 6 months old

Phil at 3 years old

The above are two members of the quartet Johnny Cash discovered. Their first big hit was "Flowers on the Wall" in 1965. (See page 160)

This 5 year old was later discovered by Conway Twitty. Some of his big hits from the sixties include: "Proud Mary," "Sweet Caroline" and "Take A Letter Maria." (See page 161)

He was 6 months old when this photo was taken. Looks like he was ready to go on the road already. He now plays guitar in the group that won the "Star Search" television show competition in 1983. Some of their hits include: "Shakin'," "Leona," and "Betty's Bein' Bad." (See page 161)

34

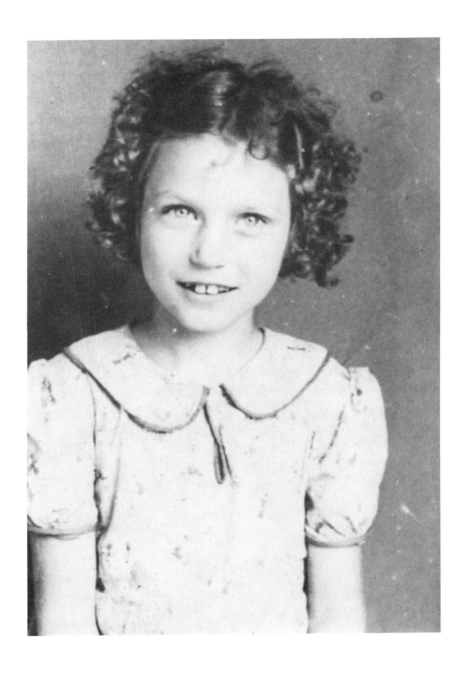

This 7 year old should be easy to guess. The film "Coal Miner's Daughter" was her life story. (See page 161)

At 3 years old she carried a baseball bat. In her teens it was a guitar. When she came to Nashville it was ability and desire. Her first PolyGram Records L.P., "From My Heart" was released in 1984. (See page 161)

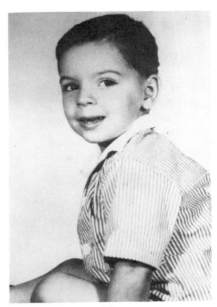

Joe at 3 years old

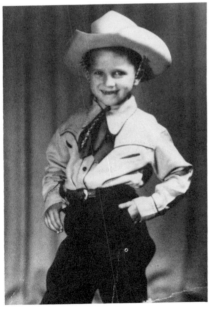

Duane at 9 years

Two members of the group that had a big hit called "Come On In" around 1979 and "Fancy Free" in 1981. (See page 162)

The 9 month old above grew up to have pop hits with Pure Prairie League. In 1984, he emerged as a solo country artist with two top ten hits, "Turn Me Loose" and "Oklahoma Borderline." (See page 162)

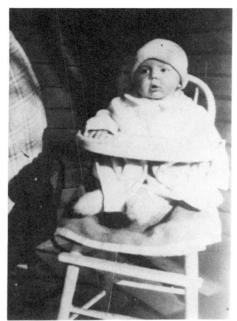

3 months and 21 days old.

He's 6 months old here and is being held by his mother, Milly.

One of his big hits was "Six Days on the Road." (See page 162)

7 years old

6 years old

Louis at 2 years old

Even his first name won't help you identify this artist. He's a regular on the "HeeHaw" tv show and in 1937 named his back-up band "The Grandchildren." (See page 162)

This photo can throw you off a bit. It was taken when he was 10 years old. 23 years later he won three Country Music Association Awards (1977). "(I'd Be) a Legend in My Time" was a big hit for him in 1974. (See page 163)

Perhaps his biggest hit was "Drift Away" in 1973, although some of his other hits were "When Your Good Love Was Mine" and "I Don't Hurt Anymore." He was 6 years old in the above photo. (See page 163)

He was 6 years old in the above photo with his mother, Bulah, and his older sister, Virgie. 37 years later he was elected into the Country Music Hall of Fame. "Four Walls" and "He'll Have to Go" were two of his biggest hits. (See page 163)

All dressed up and sitting on his father's knee, this 3 year old grew up and co-wrote the country music classic song. "Mamma's Don't Let Your Babies Grow Up To Be Cowboys." His voice has been heard on countless radio and tv commercials...and he was the sheriff on the "Maverick" tv show. (See page 163)

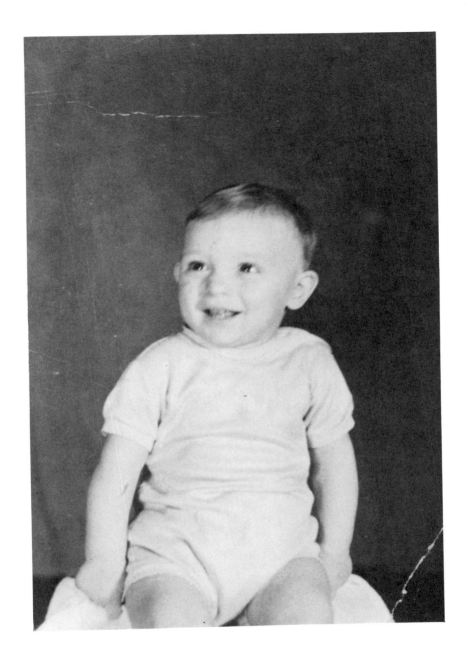

He's frequently seen on the Nashville Network's "Nashville Now" show. In 1976, he toured with the Glenn Miller Orchestra. He's 18 months old in this photo. (See page 164)

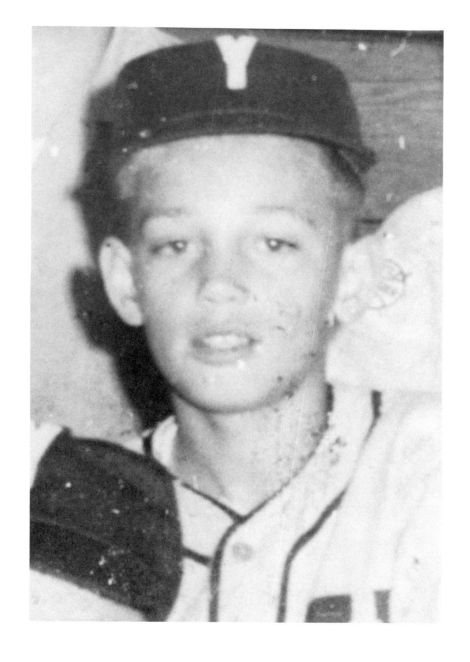

This is the youngest photo available of this artist. He's 11 years old in the above picture, which was taken from a team photo. His career erupted with his tribute to Elvis Presley in 1977. The song was called, "The King Is Gone." He's had many big hits since then. (See page 164)

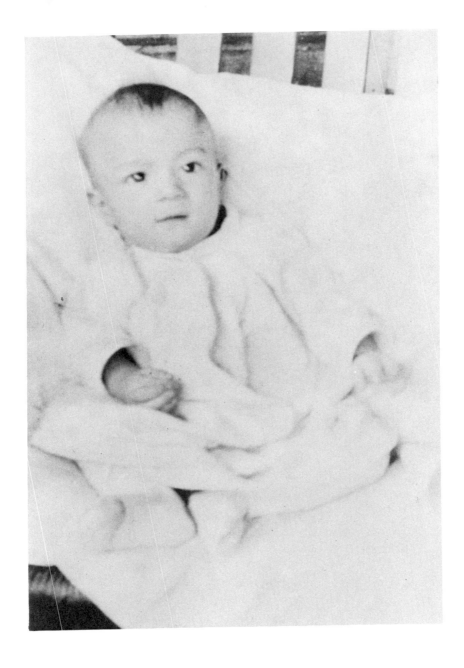

"Wine Me Up," "Occasional Wife" and "It's Four in the Morning" were some of his hits in the early seventies, which was many years after someone snapped the above photo of him at 3 months old. (See page 164)

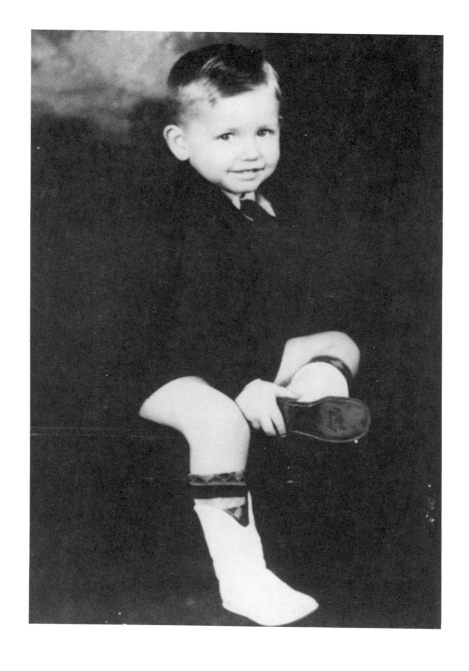

He's 5 years old here and that's about when he started playing the piano. His biggest record was "Last Date" in the early sixties. (See page 164)

There just weren't any baby photos available of this artist. He's 13 years old here. He brought brass into country music. His group won the Country Music Associations' Instrumental Group of the Year Award six straight years. (69,70,71,72,73,74) (See page 165)

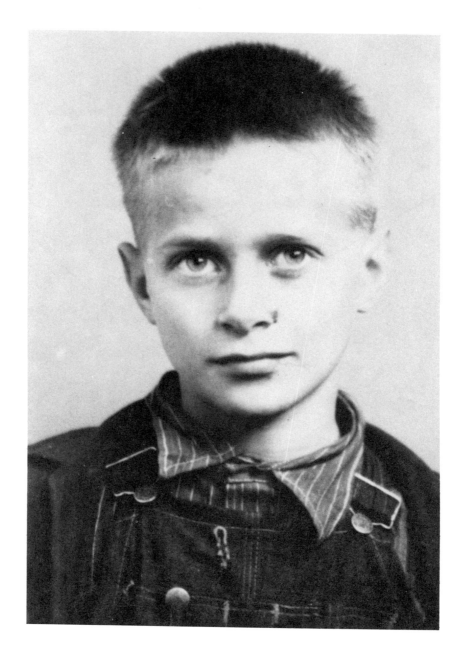

In the seventies he had several hits. "Yesterday's Gone," "Hangin' On" and "Mother Country Music" were some of them. He's 10 years old in the photo above. (See page 165)

About 5 years old here. In 1981, her CBS album, "Seven Year Ache," contained three number one country singles for her. They were: "Seven Year Ache," "Blue Moon With Heartache" and "My Baby Thinks He's a Train." (See page 165)

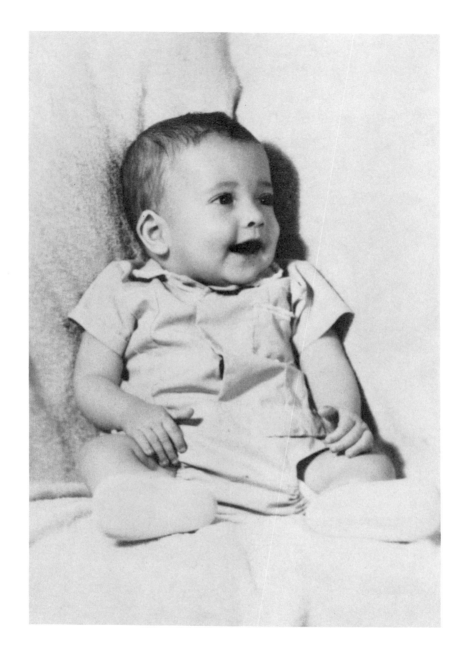

An 8 month old here, but at age 13 he was already playing road dates with his father's band, The Strangers. In the eighties, he signed with MTM Records as a solo performer. (See page 165)

Dressed here to be in her aunt's wedding, this 4 year old disrupted the ceremonies because she didn't get all the attention. She later became famous as a comedienne and joined the Grand Ole Opry in 1940. (See page 166)

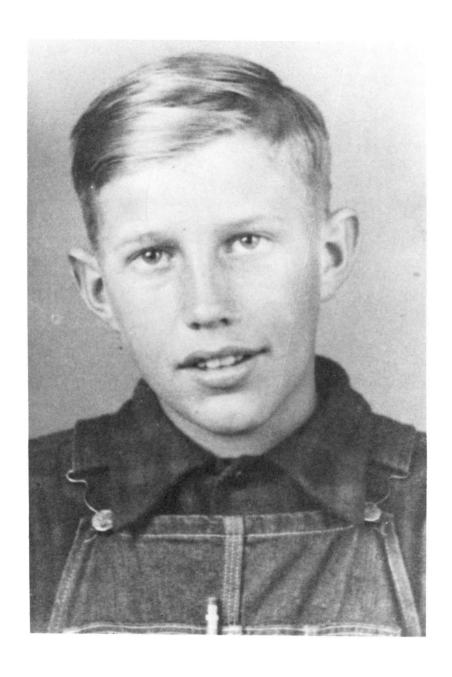

A member of the Grand Ole Opry since 1957. One of his big records was "Satisfied Mind" in 1955. In the above photo, he was 9 years old. (See page 166)

He wrote "Take Me Down" and "The Closer You Get," which were both big hits for the group, Alabama. He recorded for CBS and had "Left Side of the Bed" and "Diamond In the Dust" on the charts. He was 18 months old when this photo was snapped. (See page 166)

In 1974 he was elected into the Country Music Hall of Fame, which was 56 years after this photo was taken at age 4. He wrote "Slowpoke," "Bonaparte's Retreat" and "The Tennessee Waltz" among others. (See page 166)

A 14 month old with a guitar around his neck already. It took some time, but by the eighties he was one of the leading concert attractions and his records sales skyrocketed too! This photo's been published many times before and you should know who it is. (See page 167)

This 6 year old became known as the "Blue Jean Country Queen" in the seventies. This is a photo of her in the 1st grade. (See page 167)

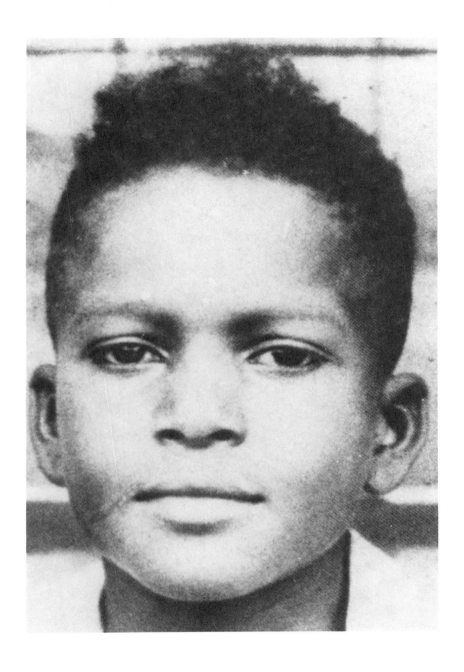

He's 11 years old here. He was born in Sledge, Mississippi. In 1966, his first record, "Snakes Crawl at Night" was released. (See page 167)

The girl in the hammock's about 8 years old. In 1982 her recording of "16th Avenue" established her as a country music star and the song as a country music classic. (See page 167)

In the early eighties some of his hits were, "Heartbroke," "Highway 40 Blues" and "Country Boy." He was just 8 months old in the above photo. (See page 168)

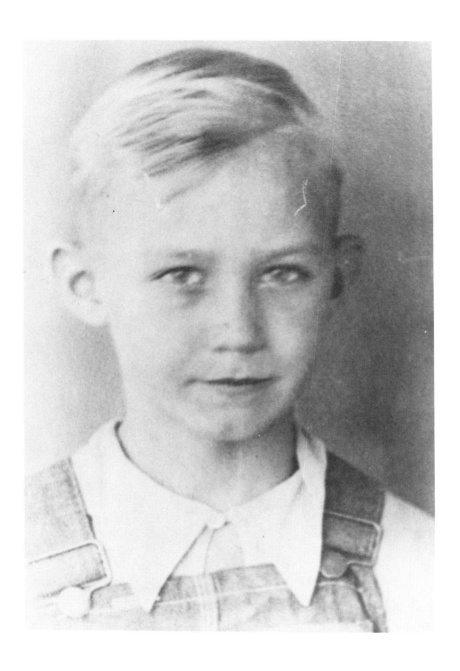

"There Goes My Everthing" was a number one country record for him. He's 5 years old in this photo. (See page 168)

The youngster in his mother's arms is just 6 months old, but he grew up to be a great country singer and an inspiration to many other country singers of today. "If You Got the Money, Honey, I Got the Time" was one of his big hits. (See page 168)

He's a proud 10 years old in this photo. He was probably just as proud when his recording of "Detroit City" became number one on all the major record charts in 1963. (See page 168)

Cindy at 1 year old

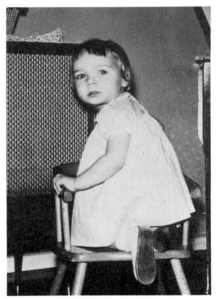

Diane at 2 years old

They're two of the foursome that rose to stardom with the hits, "Love Will Get you Through Times of No Money" and "Slow Boat to China." (See page 169)

This 2 year old mounting his wooden horse became a star in 1973 when his recording of "I Just Started Hatin' Cheatin' Songs" became a big hit. (See page 169)

He's 2 years old above, but now he's a country singer, guitarist, pianist, actor and songwriter. He wrote "Joy to the World," "Never Been to Spain" and "The Pusher," which were all very big pop records. (See page 169)

Two sweethearts dressed up for the ballet. These sisters emerged as "new wave" country artists in the mid-eighties. Kristine's 9 years old and on the left and sister Janis is 11 years old. (See page 169)

He was 9½ months old here sporting new bib overalls. In 1986, one of his big hits
was "Hell and High Water." (See page 170)

John at 5 years old

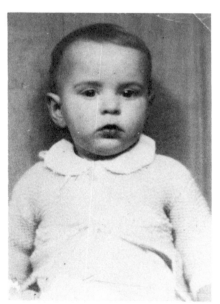

Gib at 2 months old

Although they're not really brothers, they are known as brothers. Some of their hits in the early eighties were: "She's A Friend Of A Friend," "She Belongs To Everyone But Me" and "I'm Drinking Canada Dry." (See page 170)

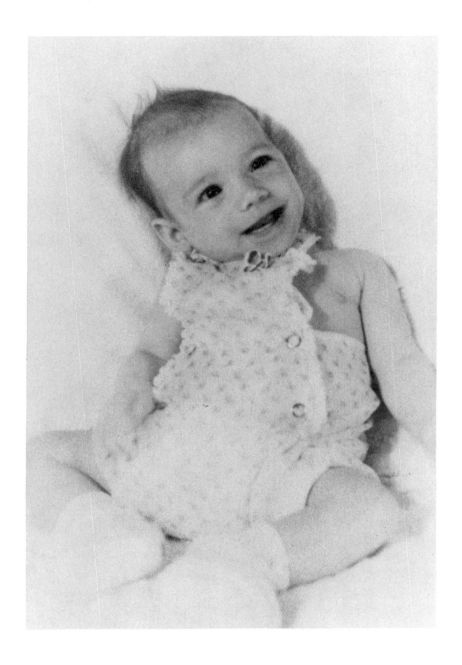

This 4 month old grew up to play bass and fiddle and played them in her older sister's band. One of *her* big hits for RCA Records was "I'm Not Through Loving You Yet." (See page 170)

71

He's 7 years old and in the 2nd grade in this photo. Two of his big hits in the sixties were "Walk on By" and "The Auctioneer." (See page 170)

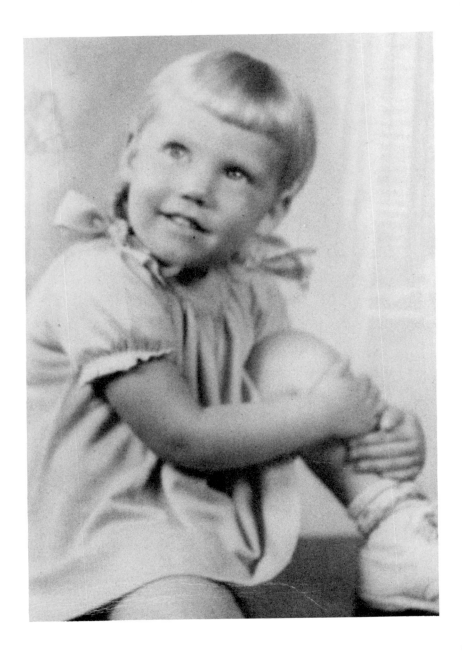

She's from Springhill, Nova Scotia and has had a very successful singing career that began in 1970 with her hit "Snowbird." She was 3 years old in this picture. (See page 171)

This is his school picture when he was 9 years old. "Roll on Big Mama" was a number one country hit for him in 1975. (See page 171)

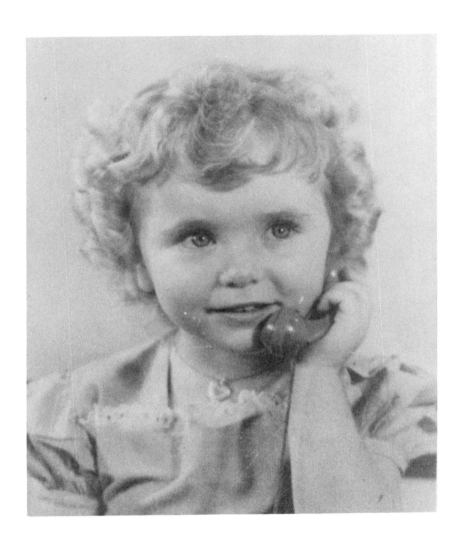

Even at 2 years old it looks like she's about to tell somebody a story like she did years later on her hit "Harper Valley PTA." (See page 171)

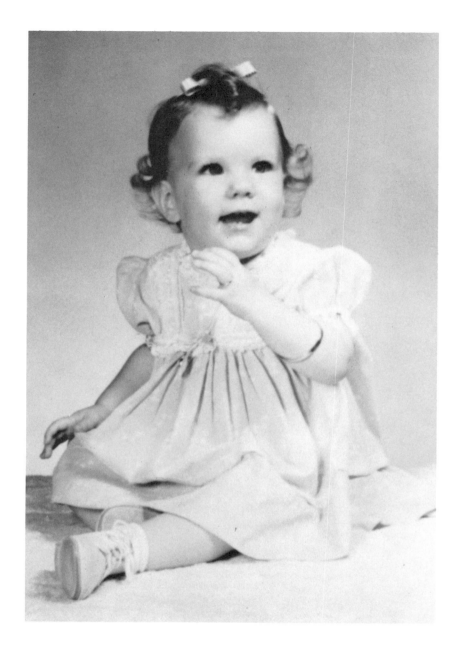

She's a Texas preacher's daughter who's first big hit was about her "Daddy's Hands."
This photo was taken when she was 10½ months old. (See page 171

He's 10 years old and you should be able to guess who this is without any clues.
(See page 172).

77

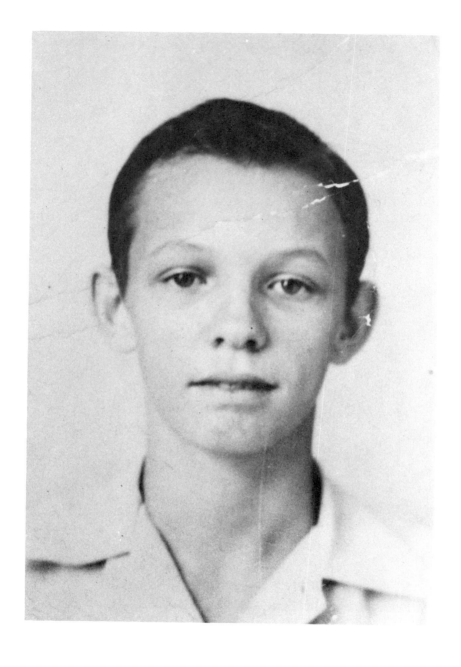

He's 14 years old here and should be easy to guess, so I'll make the clue harder. He wrote "Ruby, Don't Take Your Love to Town" and "Detroit City" among over 500 more songs. (See page 172)

As a songwriter, he wrote "Kentucky Rain," "Elvis's fiftieth gold record. As a singer, two of his big hits were "Driving My Life Away" and "Every Which Way but Loose." This photo was taken when he was 3 years old. (See page 172)

10 years old here, he later teamed up with Jack Anglin in 1938. They joined the Grand Old Opry in 1952. One of their big hits was "I Get So Lonely" in 1954. (See page 172)

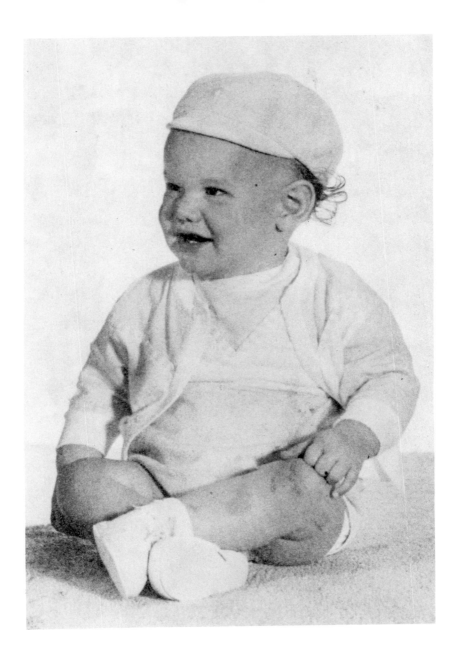

One of the hottest singers of 1986 and 1987. Some of his hits were "Diggin Up Bones," "On the Otherhand" and "1982." He was 6 months old in this photo. (See page 173)

He's on the left above, and he's 10 years old, standing with his brother, Sonny. Known as "The Mouth of Mississippi," he became well known as a comic after being a fertilizer salesman for many years. (See page 173)

A 6 year old that later became a member of the Stamps Quartet and toured with Elvis. In 1975, he formed a trio which consisted of Jackie Frantz and Vicki Hackeman. One of their big hits was "Queen of the Silver Dollar." You probably know the group's name, but what's his whole name? (See page 173)

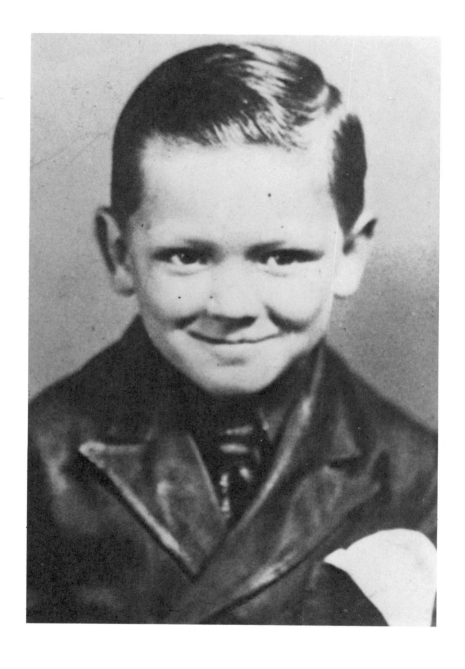

Best known for his comedy skits on "HeeHaw" and for his character, "Goober" on "The Andy Griffith" television show. He's 7 years old here. (See page 173)

Casey at 6 years old.

Liz at 4 years old with her brother Clinton.

Liz and Casey were married on May 25, 1946. Chet Atkins was the first to record Liz around 1966. Both Casey and Liz co-wrote "The Fugitive," a big hit for Merle Haggard. (See page 174)

A 5 year old cowboy and a Chevy. "You Lay So Easy on My Mind" was one of his big hits for Metromedia Records in 1973. (See page 174)

Anita at 13 years old

Helen at 18 years old

June at 13 years old

Their mother's name was Maybelle. (See page 174)

She's 7 years old in this photo. In 1985, her MCA Records release, "Lonely Days, Lonely Nights" was a hit. In the early seventies, she replaced Loretta Lynn on the Wilburn Brothers road show. (See page 174)

The 3-year old son of "The Arizona Cowboy." As a young boy of 6, he toured the rodeo, fair and theater circuit as part of his father's act. Much later he had some hit records for Warner Brothers. "Lying in My Arms" and "Never Coming Back Again" were two of them from the mid-seventies. (See page 175)

She recorded for RCA Records in the seventies and later married and toured with Merle Haggard. They have since divorced. She's 3 years old above. (See page 175)

His recording of "Jimmy Brown, the Newsboy" stayed on the top of the record charts for 33 weeks in the mid-fifties. He's been called the "Burl Ives of Bluegrass." This is how he looked at 15 months. (See page 175)

Front from left to right is Kim (6 years old), Christy (4), and in the back row it's June (8) and Kathy (10). They're really sisters from Lookout Mountain, Georgia. "I Fell In Love Again Last Night" was one of their hits in the mid-eighties. (See page 175)

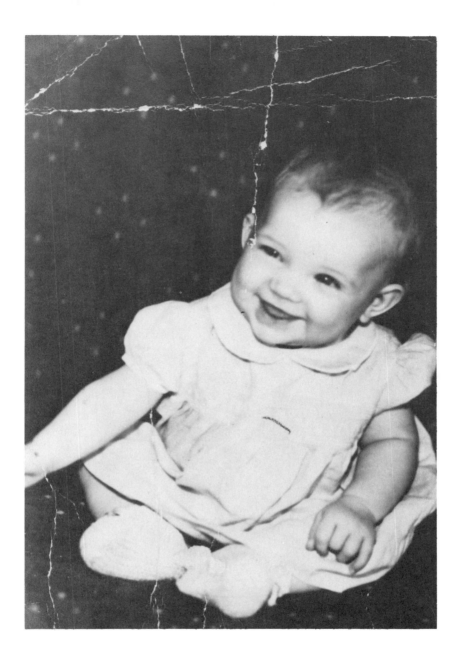

This 2 month old grew up and hosted her own NBC television show in the early eighties. In 1980, she was named The Country Music Association's Entertainer of the Year. (See page 176)

This is the *only* photo of this star as a child. It was taken when he was approximately 5 years old by a traveling photographer about 1908. This little fella grew up and became "The King of Country Music." (See page 176)

Two of his first top ten records were "Miami (my Amy)" and "Ten Feet Away" in 1985. In the photo above, he was 2 years old and already looking for an audience. (See page 176)

She's 2½ years old with the hat on and 3 years old in the other photo. In 1975, her first RCA single, "Storms Never Last" became a top ten record. Her last name was Brodt, but what was her first name? (See page 176)

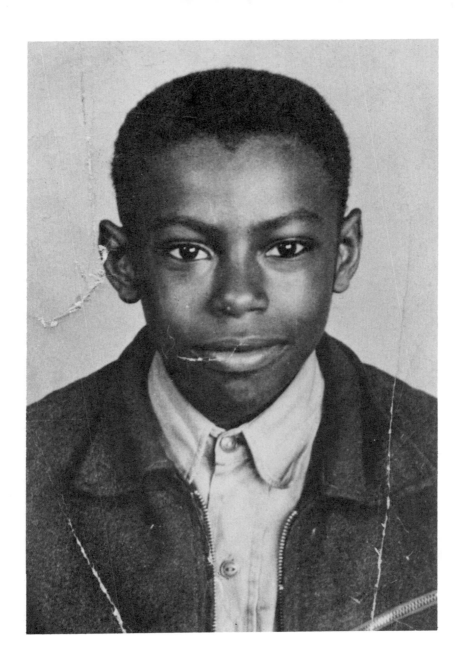

This is the only photo this artist had of himself as a boy. He's 11 years old. One of his big hits was "Don't Let the Green Grass Fool You" in the early seventies. (See page 177)

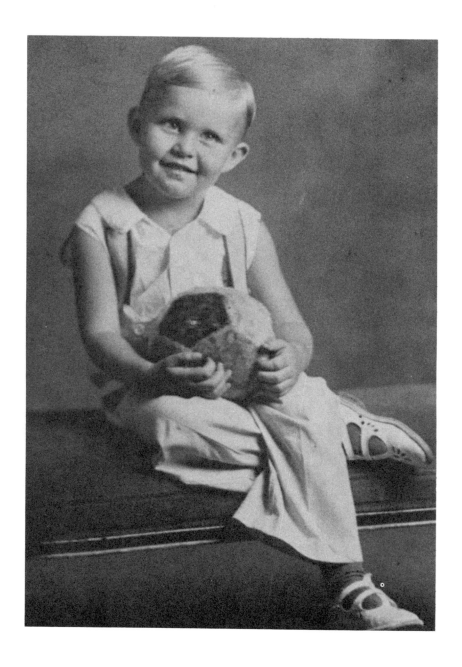

A regular cast member of the "HeeHaw" television show, his nickname was "The Round Mound of Sound." He and his wife, Donna, were the co-hosts of the Nashville Network show "Wish You Were Here." He was 3 years old when this picture was taken. (See page 177)

The little boy without a hat on the lady's lap is 8 months old. He's the father of the baby girl pictured alone. She's 1½ in the photo. They became one of the most successful father/daughter vocal teams in country music. "Heaven's Just a Sin Away" was one of their big hits. (See page 177)

"The Queen of Country Music" at 9 months old. (See page 177)

Sandy at about 2½ years.

Richard at 5 years.

They recorded a parody of The Judds hit "Mama, He's Crazy." Their's was called "Mama, She's Lazy." Another one of their parodies was "Blue Hairs Driving in My Lane," a takeoff on "Blue Eyes Crying in the Rain." (See page 178)

In the cowboy shirt photo, he's 10 years old. In the other, he's about 2 years old. The older man is Jack Prigg. Many years later, the boy in Jack's arms wrote a country music classic song about Jack. The song was "Desperados Waiting for a Train." (See page 178)

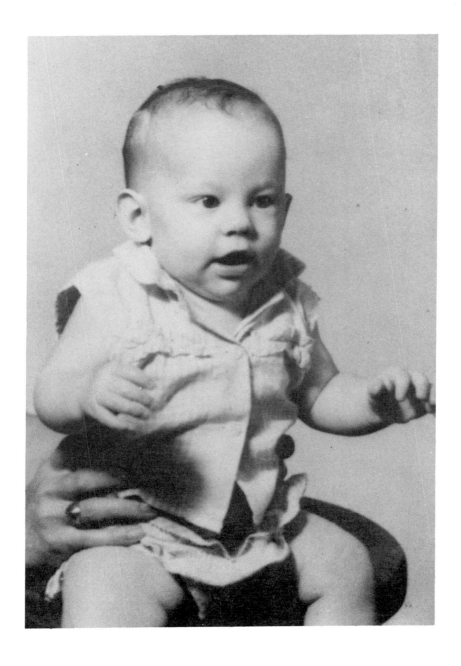

About 1 year old here. In 1984 and 1985 she was voted Country Music Association Female Vocalist of the Year and in 1986 she was named CMA Entertainer of the Year. "Little Rock" and "Whoever's in New England" were two of her number one records. (See page 178)

Celebrating 9 years old here, but a few years down the line "Rose-Colored Glasses" would become his trademark. (See page 178)

One of his big hits was "My Woman, My Woman, My Wife," which won a Grammy in 1970. "El Paso" was another one of his big hits. This is a photo of him (left) at the age of 4 with his twin sister, Mamie. (See page 179)

His great grandmother Boston is holding him. He's about 9 or 10 months old in the photo. Many years later, he and his daughters Sharon and Cheryl would have a very successful family trio. "You Put the Blue in Me" and "Hanging Around" were two of their big hits in the early eighties. (See page 179)

Just 6 months old here, but in the mid seventies her and her sister both had individual recording careers on the rise. She used only her first name and one of her big hits in 1974 was "Get On My Love Train." (See page 179)

107

The photo's a bit fuzzy, but it's the only one available of this artist. He's 3-years old here. He broke into the music business with his two brothers, Tompall and Chuck, but in the eighties became a solo star with his single of "When You're Not A Lady." (See page 179)

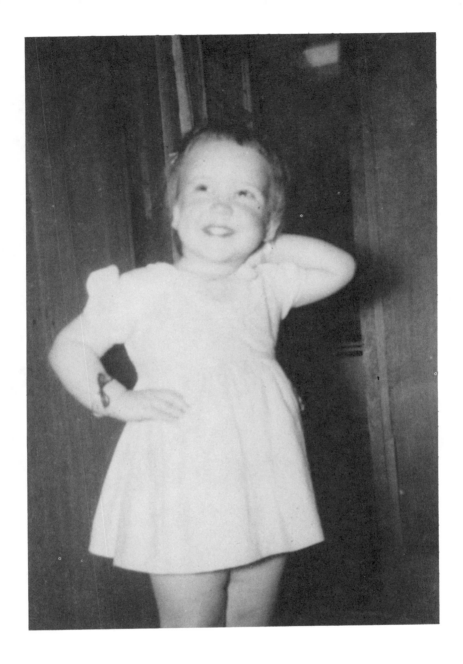

About 3 years old above, she began singing at 4 years old. At 17, she sang on a Jeno's Pizza commercial. Over the years she's done other jingles for Kellogg's, Miller Beer, Budweiser, McDonald's, Coors and Opryland. "Until I Met You" and "Girls Ride Horses Too" were two of her country hits for MTM Records in the mid-eighties. (See page 180)

The superstar is on the right and that's her sister Linda on the left. Not too many years after this photo, which shows her at 18 months, she had a hit record called "Sweet Nothin's. Many more followed. (See page 180)

The little guy in the car is 4 years old. Looks like he's ready to go on the road, which he really did on September 8, 1968, when he made his first professional appearance with his father, Marty. In the eighties he signed with Columbia Records and still plays many road dates. (See page 180)

She sang a duet with Johnnie Lee in the mid-eighties called "The Yellow Rose," which became a big hit for them and was the theme song of the NBC television show of the same name. She's about 20 months old above. (See page 180)

A 2 year old here on his way to the top. His songwriting, singing and emcee talents led him to being chosen as host of the Nashville Network's "Fandango" television show. (See page 181)

A photo of a 2 year old who's singing career started with the pop hit "Patches" in the late sixties. But by the seventies, he recorded many country hits and wrote one of the all-time country classics, "She Thinks I Still Care." (See page 181)

Some of his hits were "The Streak," "Everything Is Beautiful," and "The Mississippi Squirrel Revival." This is a photo of him at the age of 1 year. (See page 181)

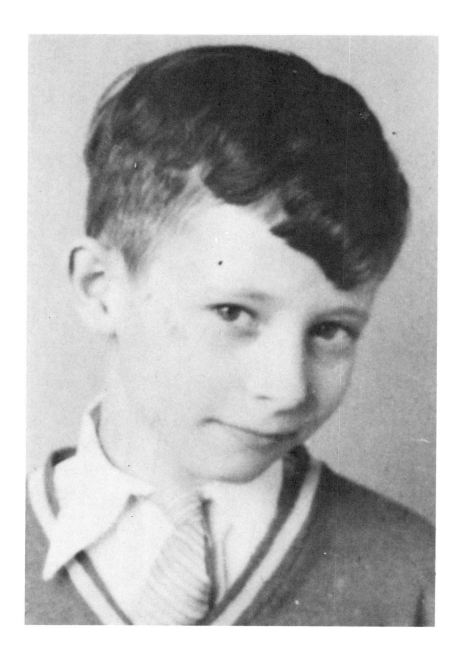

He's 8 years old above. He later became first tenor for a quartet highly associated with background singing, especially on Elvis recordings. (See page 181)

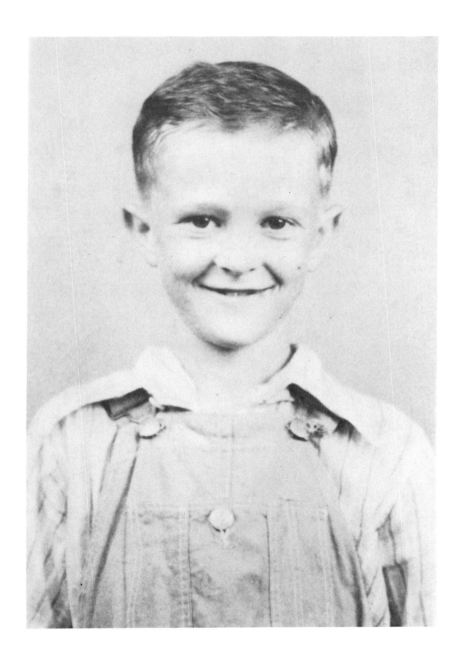

He became a writer of many hits including "9,999,999 Tears," which led to his own recording contract. One of his big hit records was "Loving Up a Storm" in 1980. In the above photo, he was 7 years old. (See page 182)

He's 4 years old in the above photo. He used to record under the name of England Dan. In 1986, he had two very big hit records, "Bop" and "Everything That Glitters (Is Not Gold)." (See page 182)

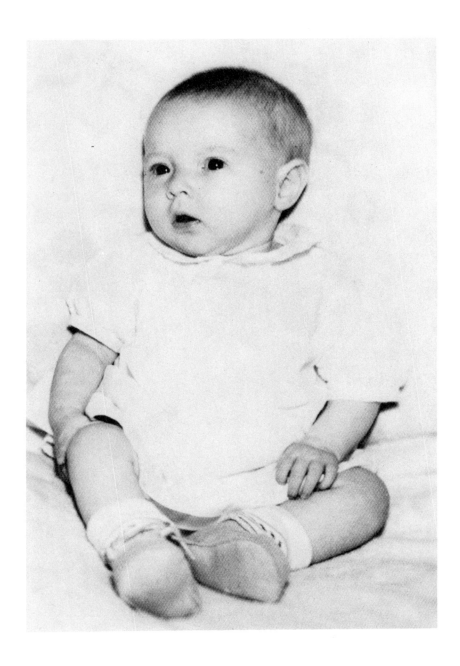

Above at 4 months old, one of her favorite things probably was a teddy bear. In 1972, it *was* definitely a teddy bear, because that was the year "The Teddy Bear Song" became a big hit for her. (See page 182)

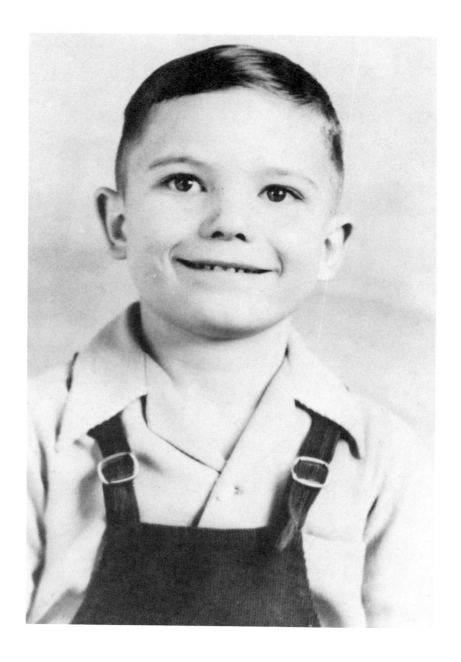

He wrote "Flowers on the Wall," which was an immediate hit in 1965 for the group he sang with at that time. He has since ventured out on his own. He was 4 years old above. (See page 182)

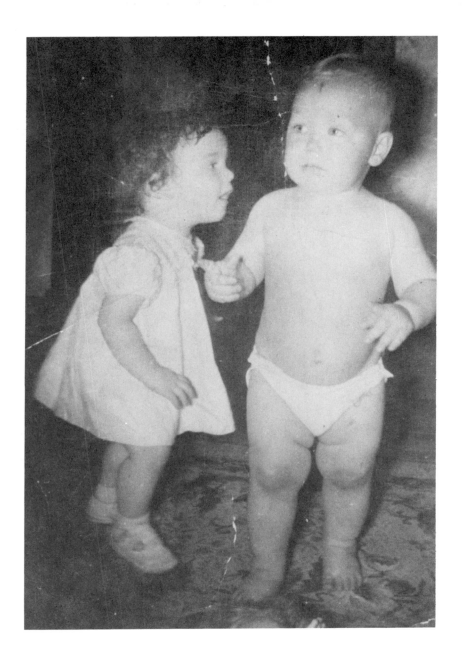

He's about 22 months old here and already has an un-identified fan watching him. He grew up and played in the bands of Dottie West and Bob Luman before branching out as a single act. One of his big hits was "Kansas City Lights" in the early eighties. (See page 183)

She became the 63rd member of the Grand Ole Opry in 1973. One of her big hits in 1974 was "Satin Sheets." She's 9 years old above. (See page 183)

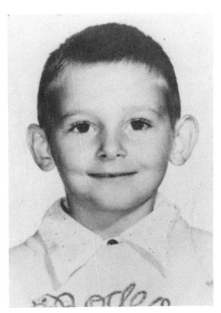

J.P. at 6 years old

Steve at about 8 years old

Lee around 6 months

Three members of a group that was founded in 1963 as a pop act, but by the eighties became a major country act. Some of their hits include: "Super Love," "Woke Up In Love" and "She's A Miracle." (See page 183)

123

Two of his big hits were, "It Turns Me Inside Out" and "Ring On Her Finger, Time On Her Hands," which were both released in the early 'eighties. In the above photo, he was 15 months old. (See page 183)

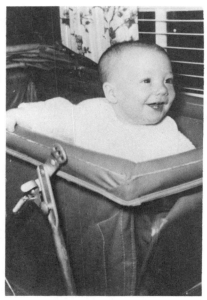

Craig at 6 months

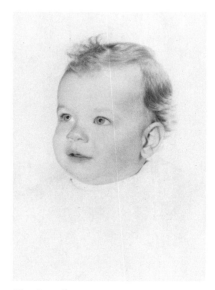

Fred at 1 year

Thom at 3 months

These three songwriters and entertainers joined forces in the mid-eighties. Their last names form the group's name. (See page 184)

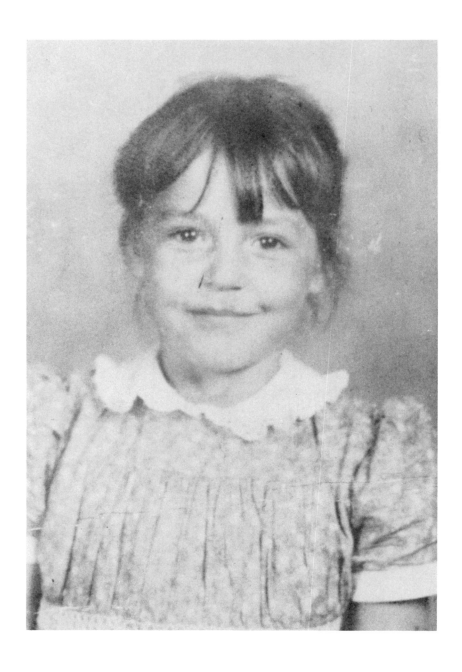

"The Happiest Girl in the Whole U.S.A." was a big hit for her in 1972. She's 5 years old in the above photo. (See page 184)

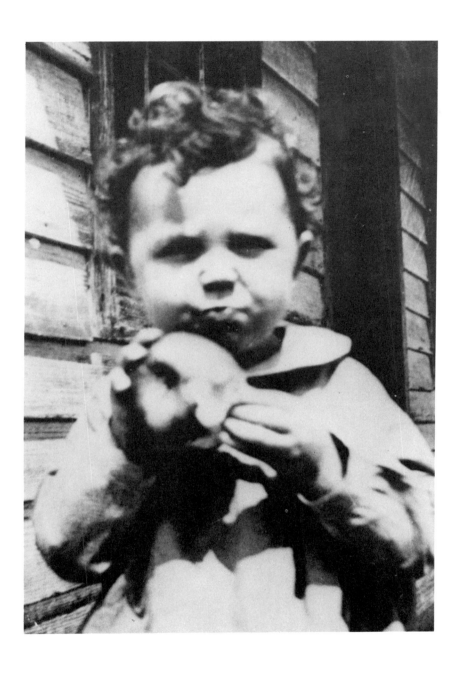

This 2 year old offering you a bite of his apple grew up to be known as "The Southern Gentleman" and one of his big hits from the sixties was "Running Bear." (See page 184)

He looks like the King of the Cowboys as a 3 year old. On the "HeeHaw" television show, Roy Clark and he sometimes do banjo duets. (See page 184)

About 12 years old here. He started his recording career around 1958. His first big hits were done with a group called The First Edition, but in the seventies his country music career soared after "Lucille" and "The Gambler." (See page 185)

His name is Greg and he's 2 ½ years old above and it looks like he's already chosen his profession. In the mid-eighties, he became part of a five-man group that had "I Want Everyone To Cry," "The Heartache Kid" and "Let The Heartache Ride" on the record charts. (See page 185)

The little guy's just 6 years old and that's his mother and father. His mother made the suit he's wearing, he told me. His nickname is "The Tennessee Plowboy." (See page 185)

Ranger Doug at 6 years old

"Too Slim" at 8 years old

Two of a trio that once hosted the "Tumbleweed Theater" on the Nashville Network and recorded for Rounder Records in the eighties. They feature old western-movie type harmony and cattle drive-seasoned humor in their stage show. (See page 185)

She was 7 years old when this photo was taken and was very fond of that little mandolin pin, which her mother gave to her. One of her big hits was "No Charge," which was released in 1974. (See page 186)

Doris at 9 months old

Tammy at 2 years old

They're two of the foursome that rose to stardom with the hits, "Love Will Get You Through Times of No Money" and "Slow Boat to China." (See page 186)

At 1 year old, perhaps he's trying to call radio stations already. He became an instant star with the song "Swingin'" in the early eighties. (See page 186)

Steve at 12 months

Richard at 9 years old

Here's two members of a quartet that was honored by the Country Music Association as Vocal Group of the Year in 1978. One of their big hits was "Elvira" in 1981. (See page 186)

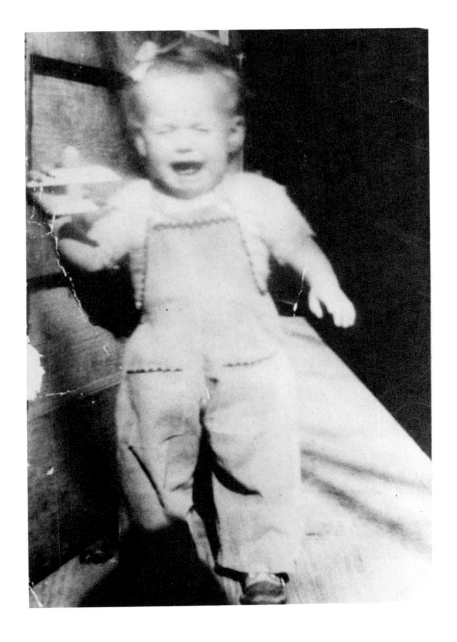

A 15 month old that looks as though she's trying to hit a very high note. Years later, RCA Records producer, Bob Ferguson, teamed her with Jim Ed Brown and they had many hit records as a duet. In 1977, they were voted Vocal Duo of the Year by the Country Music Association. Can you name her? (See page 187)

This photo was actually in two pieces when the artist found it in an old box. It shows him at about 3½ years old. He's a singer, impressionist, comedian, instrumentalist, m.c. and tv host. His Canadian television show, "Grand Old Country" won the Top Country Show of the Year award in 1977, 1978, 1979 and 1980. (See page 187)

He's 2½ years old and standing on a chair with his sister Margie beside him. This artist was the first country music artist to be honored by having his name placed in the sidewalk among the "greats" on Hollywood Boulevard in 1961. Some of his big hits were: "Gone" and "Wings Of a Dove." (See page 187)

His first number one record was "White Lightning" around 1959. He's had a bunch since then including his 1981 Grammy Award winning "He Stopped Loving Her Today." He's about 10 years old above. (See page 187)

This little guy is 3 years old here and in the mid-eighties enjoyed putting this book together. And, by the way, I hope you've enjoyed it. (See page 188)

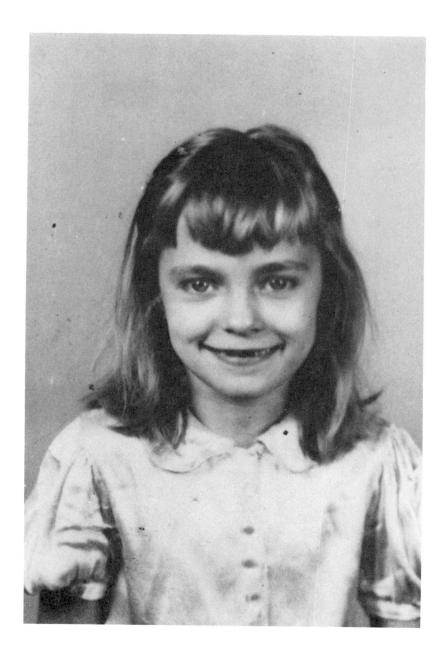

This 8 year old was one of fourteen children. Chet Atkins signed her to RCA Records in the early sixties and her first single "Once A Day" was a big hit. (See page 188)

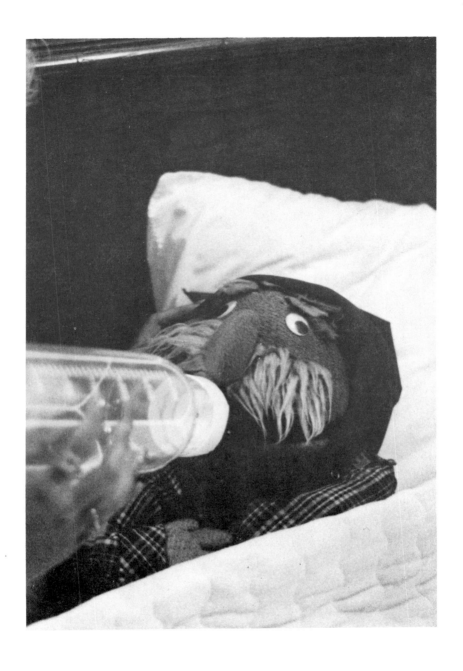

About 2 years old here, he grew up to become a very popular star on the Nashville Network. (See page 188).

Some of her big hits were "Can I Sleep In Your Arms Tonight Mister," "I Miss You" and "Don't Touch Me." She also sang hit duets with Porter Wagoner, Jack Greene and Ernest Tubb. She's just 6 months old above. (See page 188).

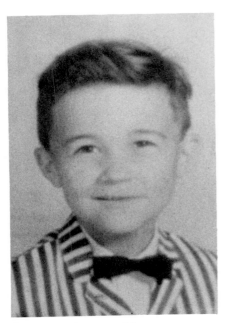

Jimmy at 6 years old

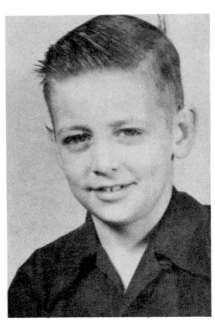

Don at 8 years old

Don and Jimmy are now two members of a very popular country music quartet, which won the Country Music Association's Vocal Group of the Year award nine straight years (1972-1980). (See page 189)

One of his big hits was "Almost Persuaded" in 1966. His ancestors include Robert E. Lee and Sam Houston. In this photo he was 3 years old. (See page 189)

A 2 year old destined for a future in country music tries her hand at playing her daddy Mel's guitar. (See page 189)

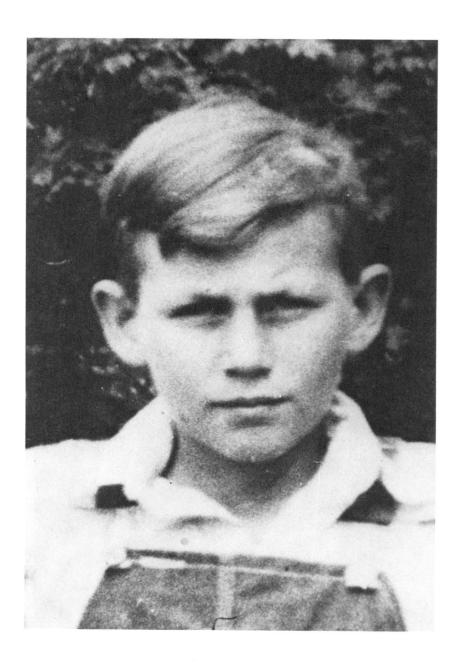

One of his first recordings for RCA was a vocal called "Don't Hand Me That Line,"
but he really became known for his guitar playing. He's 9 years old here. (See page 189)

3 year old Jeff

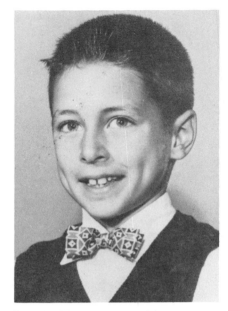

Jimmie F. at 5 years old

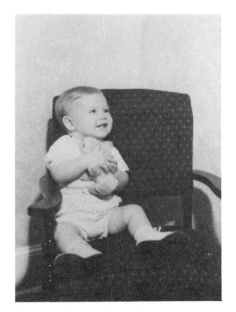

Bob at 18 months old

Jimmy I. at 9 years

Here's four of the five members of this group. Their 1972 album, "Will The Circle Be Unbroken" is recognized by the *Nashville Tennessean* as one of the most important recordings in the history of the Nashville music business. (See page 190)

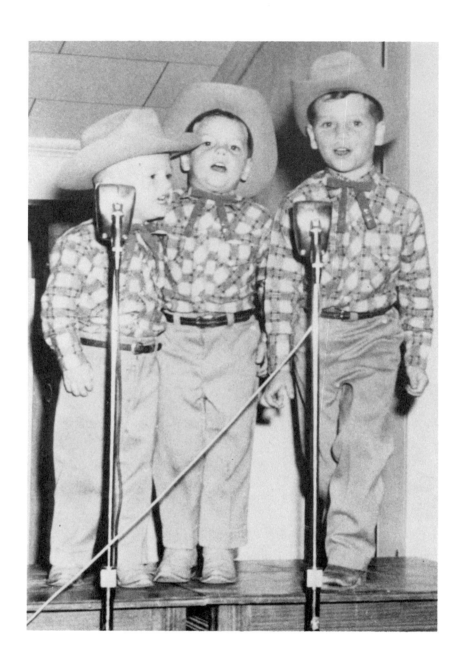

According to CBS Records, (who provided this photo) they range in age from 5 years old to 9. Larry's the tallest, Rudy's the smallest and Steve's in the middle. "All the Gold in California" was one of their big hits in 1980. (See page 190)

COUNTRY MUSIC LOVERS!

If you're looking for other books about country music, the artists and the music industry, Union and Confederacy, Inc. can help. We've got 'em all!

Send $1.25 for our current book list. We've got some great titles and some great buys.

Our address is: UNION AND CONFEDERACY, INC.
P. O. Box 11
College Grove, Tennessee 37046

A N D

Be sure to include your name and address so we know where to send the book list.

Additional copies of this publication can be obtained by sending $10.95 (which includes postage and handling) to:

Union and Confederacy Inc.
P. O. Box 11
College Grove, Tennessee 37046

Be sure to include *your* name and address when ordering.

Page 2 Artist   Gary Morris

Page 1 Artist   Do-Rite Irlene Mandrell

Page 3 Artist

Lafayette, Louisiana native Eddy Raven

Page 4 Artist

Virginia Ruth Watson's little brother Gene Watson.

Page 5 Artist David Frizzell

Page 6 Artist Glen Campbell

Page 7 Artist   Margo Smith

Page 8 Artist
Grand Ole Opry Star Jan Howard

Page 9 Artist Tammy Wynette

Page 10 Artist Bob Luman

Page 11 Artist
"You Can Be A Star" host Jim Ed Brown

Page 12 Artist Marty Stuart

Page 13 Artist

The two sisters of The Whites.
Above: Sharon (left) and Cheryl (right)

Page 14 Artist Tanya Tucker

Page 15 Artist

"HeeHaw" performers Jim and John Hager,
better known as The Hagers. (Jim's on the
left in this photo.)

Page 16 Artist   Willie Nelson

156

Page 17 Artist

Singer of "Sixteen Tons" Tennessee Ernie Ford

Page 18 Artist Del Reeves

Page 19 Artist The Judds

Mother Naomi, above on the left sings harmony and daughter Wynonna (right) sings lead and plays guitar.

Page 20 Artist Little Jimmy Dickens

Page 21 Artist   Johnny Rodriguez

Page 22 Artist   Penny DeHaven

Page 23 Artist

Country Music Hall of Fame Member
Red Foley

Page 24 Artist   Freddy Weller

Page 25 Artist   Sylvia

Page 26 Artist   Dolly Parton

Page 27 Artist   Johnny Bright Russell

Page 28 Artist   Robin Lee

Page 29 Artist   B. J. Thomas

Page 30 Artist   Mel McDaniels

Page 31 Artist   Lynn Anderson

Page 32 Artist

The Statler Brothers
Front row, left to right is Phil Balsley, and
Jimmy Fortune. Back row left to right is
Harold Reid and Don Reid.

Page 33 Artist

Anthony Armstrong Jones

Page 34 Artist

It's Bobby Randall of Sawyer Brown
Left to right: Joe Smyth, Bobby Randall,
Mark Miller, Jim Scholten & Greg
Hubbard

Page 35 Artist

Coal Miner's Daughter Loretta Lynn

Page 36 Artist   Kathy Mattea

Page 37 Artist

The Oak Ridge Boys
(Left to right) Duane Allen, Joe Bonsall,
Steve Sanders and Richard Sterban

Page 38 Artist   Vince Gill

Page 39 Artist   Dave Dudley

Page 40 Artist   Louis Marshall Jones
"Grandpa Jones"

162

Page 41 Artist Ronnie Milsap

Page 42 Artist Narvel Felts

Page 43 Artist
Country Music Hall of Fame Member Jim
Reeves

Page 44 Artist Ed Bruce

Page 45 Artist Tom Grant

Page 46 Artist Ronnie McDowell

Page 47 Artist   Faron Young

Page 48 Artist   Floyd Cramer

Page 49 Artist

Danny Davis, leader of the Nashville Brass

Page 50 Artist   Vern Gosdin

Page 51 Artist   Rosanne Cash

Page 52 Artist   Marty Haggard

Page 53 Artist   Minnie Pearl

Page 54 Artist Porter Wagoner

Page 55 Artist Mark Gray

Page 56 Artist

Country Music Hall of Fame member Pee
Wee King

Page 57 Artist Hank Williams Jr.

Page 58 Artist Linda Hargrove

Page 59 Artist Charley Pride

Page 60 Artist Lacy J. Dalton

Page 61 Artist Ricky Skaggs

Page 62 Artist
The Jolly Giant, Jack Greene

Page 63 Artist Lefty Frizzell

Page 64 Artist Bobby Bare

Page 65 Artist

The Girls Next Door
(Left to right) Tammy Stephens, Diane
Williams, Doris King and Cindy Nixon

Page 66 Artist Moe Bandy

Page 67 Artist Hoyt Axton

Page 68 Artist
The Sweethearts of the Rodeo
Above: Janis (l) and Kristine (r)

Page 70 Artist   The Burrito Brothers
Left: Gib Guilbeau
Right: John Beland

Page 69 Artist T. Graham Brown

Page 71 Artist Louise Mandrell

Page 72 Artist   Leroy Van Dyke

Page 73 Artist Anne Murray

Page 74 Artist Joe Stampley

Page 75 Artist Jeannie C. Riley

Page 76 Artist Holly Dunn

Page 77 Artist   Johnny Cash

Page 78 Artist   Mel Tillis

Page 79 Artist Eddie Rabbitt

Page 80 Artist

Johnny Wright of Johnnie and Jack

172

Page 81 Artist Randy Travis

Page 82 Artist Jerry Clower

Page 83 Artist

The group's name is Dave and Sugar and
his name is David Rowland

Page 84 Artist George Lindsey

173

Page 85 Artist

Casey and Liz Anderson

Page 86 Artist   Bobby G. Rice

Page 87 Artists

The Carter Sisters
Mother Maybelle Carter (sitting) with her
three daughters June (left), Anita (center)
and Helen.

Page 88 Artist Patty Loveless

Page 89 Artist   Rex Allen Jr.

Page 90 Artist Leona Williams

Page 91 Artist   Mac Wiseman

Page 92 Artists

The Forester Sisters

Kim

Christy   June

Kathy

175

Page 93 Artist   Barbara Mandrell

Page 94 Artist

Grand Ole Opry and Country Music Hall of Fame member Roy Acuff

Page 95 Artist Keith Whitley

Page 96 Artist Dottsy

Page 97 Artist O. B. McClinton

Page 98 Artist Kenny Price

Page 100 Artist Kitty Wells

Page 99 Artist

The Kendalls (Royce & Jeannie)
Note—In the photo on page 99, left to
right: Floyce Kendall, Mrs. Viola Kendall,
a Mrs. Cook with Royce Kendall on her
lap. Mrs. Kendall is the mother of Floyce
and Royce.

Page 102 Artist   Guy Clark

Page 101 Artist

Sandy (left) and Richard of Pinkard and Bowden

Page 103 Artist Reba McEntire

Page 104 Artist   John Conlee

Page 105 Artist   Marty Robbins

Page 106 Artist

Buck White of The Whites

Page 107 Artist   LaCosta (Tucker)

Page 108 Artist Jim Glaser

Page 109 Artist Judy Rodman

Page 110 Artist Brenda Lee

Page 111 Artist Ronnie Robbins

Page 112 Artist Lane Brody

Page 114 Artist Dickey Lee

Page 113 Artist Bill Anderson

Page 116 Artist

He's first tenor Gordon Stoker of The Jordanaires. Left to right: Stoker, Neal Matthews, Duane West and Ray Walker

Page 115 Artist Ray Stevens

Page 117 Artist   Razzy Bailey

Page 118 Artist Dan Seals

Page 119 Artist Barbara Fairchild

Page 120 Artist

Former Statler Brother Lew DeWitt

Page 121 Artist Steve Wariner

Page 122 Artist Jeanne Pruett

Page 123 Artist

Exile
Left to right: Lee Carroll, Steve
Goetzman, J. P. Pennington, Sonny
Lemaire and Les Taylor

Page 124 Artist Lee Greenwood

Page 125 Artist

Schuyler, Knobloch & Bickhardt
Left to right: Fred Knobloch, Craig
Bickhardt and Thom Schuyler

Page 126 Artist   Donna Fargo

Page 127 Artist   Sonny James

Page 128 Artist

Banjo playin' Buck Trent

Page 129 Artist   Kenny Rogers

Page 130 Artist

Restless Heart
Greg Jennings is the fourth from the left.
Other members (left to right) are: Larry
Stewart, Paul Gregg, David Innis and John
Dittrich

Page 131 Artist

Country Music Hall of Fame member
Eddy Arnold

Page 132 Artist
Riders In The Sky
Kneeling is "Too Slim" LaBour. Standing
left to right is Ranger Doug Green and
Woody Paul Chrisman.

Page 134 Artist

The Girls Next Door
(Left to right) Cindy Nixon, Tammy
Stephens, Doris King and Diane Williams

Page 133 Artist   Melba Montgomery

Page 136 Artist

The Oak Ridge Boys
(Left to right) Duane Allen, Joe Bonsall,
Steve Sanders and Richard Sterban

Page 135 Artist   John Anderson

186

Page 137 Artist   Helen Cornelius

Page 138 Artist   Ronnie Prophet

Page 139 Artist   Ferlin Husky

Page 140 Artist
"The Possum" George Jones

Page 141 Artist

Author of this book, Paul Randall

Page 142 Artist Connie Smith

Page 143 Artist   Shotgun Red

Page 144 Artist   Jeannie Seely

Page 145 Artist

The Statler Brothers
Front row, left to right is Phil Balsley and
Harold Reid. Back row, left to right is Don
Reid and Jimmy Fortune.

Page 146 Artist   David Houston

Page 147 Artist   Pam Tillis

Page 148 Artist

"Mr. Guitar" Chet Atkins

Page 149 Artist   The Nitty Gritty Dirt Band
                    Left to right: Jimmy Ibbotson, Bob
                    Carpenter, Bernie Leadon, Jimmy Fadden
                    and Jeffa Hanna

Page 150 Artist   The Gatlins
                   Left to right: Rudy, Larry and Steve

Autographs

Autographs